SO
You Want to Start Investing

Copyright ©2025 by SO Book Series. All rights reserved.

No part of this book may be reproduced, stored in a retrieval system, or transmitted in any form or by any means electronic, mechanical, photocopying, recording, or otherwise, without the prior written permission of the publisher, except in the case of brief quotations embodied in critical articles or reviews.

This book is a work of non-fiction. All efforts have been made to ensure the accuracy of the information presented. However, the author and publisher are not liable for errors, omissions, or any outcomes resulting from the use of this material.

Contents

INTRODUCTION 6
   Shifting from Saving to Growing Wealth 7
   The Power of Compounding: Time is Your Best Ally 9
   Not Sure Where to Begin? Start Here. 12
PART ONE 13
   Understanding Risk and Reward 14
   The Risk-Return Trade-off: What It Means for You 14
   Common Myths About Investing-Debunked 17
   Building a Strong Financial Base 21
   Do You Need an Emergency Fund Before Investing? 21
   Managing Debt: A Prerequisite for Success 23
   Budgeting with an Investor's Perspective 25
   Setting Clear Investment Goals 27
   Short-Term vs. Long-Term Investing: Understanding the Trade-offs 28
   Defining Your Risk Tolerance: How Much Uncertainty Can You Handle? 30
   Aligning Investments with Life Milestones 32
   Don't Let These Myths Hold You Back 36

Build Your Foundation First 38

PART TWO 39

Navigating the Investment Landscape 40

Breaking Down Investment Options 40

Stocks, Bonds, and Beyond: What Are Your Choices? 41

Bonds: Stability in Volatile Times 42

Real Estate, Crypto, and Alternative Investments: Worth the Hype? 43

Alternative Investments: Diversification Beyond the Norm . 44

ETFs vs. Mutual Funds: What's Right for You? 45

How the Market Works 46

Understanding Bull and Bear Markets 47

How Interest Rates and Inflation Shape Investing Strategies 49

The Role of Economic Cycles in Smart Investing 51

The Psychology of Investing 53

Fear, Greed, and Market Volatility 53

Avoiding Common Pitfalls Like FOMO and Panic Selling 55

Emotional Discipline: The Key to Long-Term Wealth 56

Choosing the Right Investment Type: What to Consider 58

PART THREE 61

Crafting Your Strategy 62

The Importance of Diversification 62

Passive vs. Active Investing: Which Suits You? 63

Pound-Cost Averaging: A Simple Yet Powerful Strategy 66

Tax and Your Investments: What You Need to Know 68

The Taxes Investors Face 68

Tax-Efficient Strategy Tip 70

Making Smart Decisions in Any Market 71

When to Buy, Hold, or Sell 71

Understanding Market Trends and Indicators 74

Leveraging Technology and Resources in Investing 75

Investment Apps and Robo-Advisors: Do They Work? 76

Learning from the Best: Books, Podcasts, and Experts to Follow 81

PART FOUR 85

The Power of Compound Growth 86

Real Stories of Everyday Investors Who Built Wealth Over Time 86

How to Stay Patient and Consistent 89

Adapting to Life Changes and Market Shifts 90

Investing Through Recessions and Economic Uncertainty .. 91

Adjusting Your Portfolio as You Age 92

Preparing for Retirement: Passive Income and Withdrawal Strategies.. 94

Beyond Money: Investing in Yourself 95

Financial Knowledge as Your Greatest Asset......................... 96

The Intersection of Investing and Entrepreneurship 97

Why True Wealth Is More Than Just Numbers...................... 99

Your Investing Action Plan: A Recap for Moving Forward .. 101

CONCLUSION.. 106

Glossary of Key Investing Terms (Plain-English Edition)..... 108

INTRODUCTION

Many people believe investing is only for the wealthy – a financial playground reserved for those with millions to spare. It's a common myth, and one that stops many people from ever getting started. In truth, investing is one of the most effective ways to build wealth, regardless of your starting point. The stock market doesn't care how much is in your bank account. It rewards knowledge, not net worth. Whether you're investing £100 or £1 million, the rules are the same.

Consider this: in 1980, if you had invested just £1,000 into the S&P 500 – a major US stock market index tracking 500 of the largest American companies – that investment would have grown to over £160,000 by now. No hedge funds, no insider trading, just the simple act of putting money into the market and letting it work for you over time. Compare that to leaving money in a traditional savings account. With inflation constantly eroding purchasing power, a savings account today often yields less than 1% interest, while historical stock market returns average around 7-10% annually.

Wealth isn't a prerequisite for investing; instead, investing is the bridge that helps everyday people build wealth. With the rise of commission-free trading apps and fractional shares, starting an investment journey no longer requires thousands of pounds. Even with £10 or £20, you can begin accumulating assets and watching your money grow. The key is shifting your mindset from "I need money to invest" to "Investing is how I build money."

Shifting from Saving to Growing Wealth

For generations, financial wisdom revolved around saving: stash money away, avoid risk, and let time do the rest. But saving alone doesn't make you wealthy; it simply preserves what you already have. In contrast, investing takes the same principle of patience and supercharges it with growth potential.

Think of saving and investing as two different paths leading toward financial security. Saving is like walking. You move forward slowly and steadily, but progress is limited. Investing, on the other hand, is like riding a bicycle. It might feel risky at first, but once you gain balance, your speed increases dramatically. The difference? Knowledge and discipline.

A classic example of this shift in mindset is Warren Buffett, who bought his first stock at 11 years old. He didn't have an enormous sum of money, but he understood something critical: money has the potential to multiply when put in the right place. Instead of parking cash in a bank, he put it to work in businesses that generated returns. Today, that principle remains unchanged. Whether you're buying shares of a Fortune 500 company or investing in a diversified index fund, the goal is the same: let money work for you instead of you constantly working for money.

It's also important to acknowledge the psychology behind saving versus investing. Saving feels safe; investing can feel risky. But, in reality, failing to invest is often the riskiest move of all. Inflation, which averages around 2-3% annually, steadily reduces the value of cash over time. That means a £100,000 savings account today might only have the purchasing power of £80,000 in a couple of decades. Investing, however, offers the potential not just to keep up with inflation but to significantly outpace it.

The shift from saving to growing wealth starts with education. Understanding risk, diversification, and long-term strategies allows individuals to invest with confidence. Instead of focusing solely on preserving money, a wealth-building mindset prioritises making money work smarter and harder over time.

The Power of Compounding: Time is Your Best Ally

If there's one concept every investor should grasp early on, it's the power of compounding. Albert Einstein reportedly called compound interest "the eighth wonder of the world," and for good reason. It's the secret sauce that turns small investments into substantial wealth over time.

Compounding is simple: when your investments generate returns, those returns are reinvested, allowing future returns to be calculated on a larger base. This creates a snowball effect, where even modest contributions can lead to significant wealth if given enough time.

Let's break it down with an example. Imagine two investors: Sarah and Tom. Sarah starts investing at 25, putting away £4,000 annually into a low-cost index fund – perhaps through a Stocks & Shares ISA – earning an average annual return of 8%. She does this for 20 years and then stops contributing altogether. Tom, on the other hand, waits until he's 40 to begin, but contributes the same £4,000 annually for 25 years at the same 8% return. By the time they both reach 65, who has more money?

Despite contributing for fewer years, Sarah comes out ahead. Her early start allowed compounding to work in her favour, and her portfolio grows significantly larger than Tom's by retirement. The reason? Time. The longer an investment has to grow, the more powerful compounding becomes.

Compounding isn't just about retirement accounts. It applies to dividends reinvested into stocks, interest earned on bonds, and even reinvesting profits back into a business. The key takeaway? Starting early, even with small amounts, is far more impactful than waiting for the "perfect time" to begin investing.

One of the best examples of compounding in action is Berkshire Hathaway, Warren Buffett's company. Buffett's fortune wasn't built overnight it was the result of consistent investing, reinvesting, and letting compounding work its magic over decades. His wealth accumulation was relatively slow at first, but once the snowball effect kicked in, it grew exponentially.

The same principle applies to everyday investors. Whether you're investing £50 a month or £5,000, the earlier you begin, the more time compounding has to work in your favour. It's not about timing the market; it's about time *in* the market.

Not Sure Where to Begin? Start Here.

If you're new to investing, don't worry. Here's a simple path to get you started without feeling stressed or overwhelmed:

☐ Open a Stocks & Shares ISA

Start with a platform like Vanguard, AJ Bell, or Hargreaves Lansdown. It's tax-efficient and easy to manage.

☐ Pick a Simple Fund

Look for a low-cost, global index fund or ETF (e.g. FTSE All-World or S&P 500 tracker). You don't need to pick individual stocks.

☐ Set Up a Monthly Contribution

Even £25 or £50 a month is enough to begin. Automate it so you don't have to think about it.

☐ Focus on Learning, Not Perfection

You don't need to know everything. You just need to start—and stay curious.

☐ Give It Time

Think in years, not weeks. Your future self will thank you.

PART ONE

Understanding Risk and Reward

Investing is often painted as a thrilling yet intimidating journey. On the one hand, it promises the tantalising potential of financial freedom. On the other, it carries the possibility of loss. This delicate dance between gains and losses is where the concept of risk and reward takes centre stage. For anyone serious about building wealth through investing, understanding this balance is crucial.

The Risk-Return Trade-off: What It Means for You

At its core, the risk-return trade-off is a fundamental principle in investing: the higher the potential return of an investment, the greater the risk involved. There are no guarantees in the market, and even seemingly "safe" investments carry their own set of risks, whether it's inflation eroding purchasing power or economic downturns impacting bond yields.

Consider the contrast between two common investment options: government bonds and stocks. A UK government bond (known as a gilt), often considered a low-risk investment, offers relatively modest but stable returns. On the other hand, investing in the shares of a fast-growing tech startup could lead to substantial gains – or significant losses if the company underperforms. This spectrum of risk and reward is something every investor must learn to navigate.

One way to visualise this is through historical data. Over the past century, the S&P 500 – which represents a broad cross-section of major US companies – has delivered average annual returns of around 10%. However, that return doesn't come in a straight line. Some years deliver double-digit gains, while others bring sharp declines. That's the trade-off. Long-term investors who stay the course through market ups and downs tend to see growth over time. But short-term traders risk losses if they buy in at the wrong moment.

Another important element of risk is volatility, or how much an investment's price fluctuates over time. High-volatility assets like cryptocurrencies or early-stage startups can swing dramatically in value, making them both exciting and nerve-wracking. More stable assets, like blue-chip stocks or dividend-paying companies, tend to experience smaller price movements, offering a smoother ride for risk-averse investors.

Understanding the risk-return trade-off isn't about avoiding risk entirely, it's about managing it effectively. A diversified portfolio spreads your risk across different types of investments, so a single failure won't derail your progress. Likewise, a long-term mindset helps you ride out short-term market swings and take full advantage of compounding growth.

Common Myths About Investing-Debunked

When it comes to investing, misinformation is rampant. Many people hold on to long-standing myths that prevent them from making informed decisions. Let's break down some of the most common misconceptions and uncover the reality behind them.

✗ Myth 1: Investing Is Only for the Wealthy

For years, investing was seen as an exclusive club reserved for the rich. But the financial world has changed. Today, with the rise of commission-free trading apps, robo-advisors, and fractional shares, virtually anyone can start investing with as little as £5. The barrier to entry has never been lower.

The key isn't how much money you start with — it's consistency. Even small, regular investments into a diversified portfolio can grow into substantial wealth over time, thanks to the power of compounding. Take someone who invests £100 a month into a low-cost index fund through a Stocks & Shares ISA. Over 30 years, assuming an average annual return of 10%, that investment could grow to over £200,000. The secret isn't a big lump sum — it's time, patience, and sticking with the plan.

✗ Myth 2: The Stock Market Is Just Like Gambling

It's easy to see why people compare investing to gambling – both involve risk, and both can lead to gains or losses. But beyond that surface similarity, they're fundamentally different. Gambling is based on chance, with the odds typically stacked against you. Investing, by contrast, is about making informed, strategic decisions rooted in research, data, and long-term thinking.

When you invest in a company, you're buying a stake in a real business – one that generates income, employs people, and creates goods or services. If the business grows, so does the value of your investment. Over time, successful companies tend to increase in value, and investors benefit from that growth.

Unlike gambling, investing offers ways to manage and reduce risk. Through diversification, asset allocation, and other strategies, you can spread your investments and limit potential losses. In a casino, there's no equivalent. Once your money's on the table, the outcome is out of your hands.

✗ Myth 3: You Need to Time the Market to Succeed

One of the biggest mistakes new investors make is believing they need to predict market movements perfectly to be successful. This often leads to paralysis by analysis, where potential investors wait endlessly for the "perfect" time to buy, only to miss out on long-term gains.

The truth? Even professional investors struggle to time the market consistently. Instead, one of the most proven strategies for success is pound-cost averaging (PCA), investing a fixed amount at regular intervals, regardless of market conditions. This approach smooths out volatility and eliminates the stress of trying to buy at the perfect moment.

✗ Myth 4: Investing Is Too Complicated for Beginners

While investing does have complexities, the idea that it's too difficult for beginners is outdated. With the abundance of educational resources available today, investment podcasts, online courses, and user-friendly platforms, it's easier than ever to get started.

Many successful investors follow straightforward strategies that don't require advanced financial knowledge. Index investing, for example, allows investors to passively track the market's performance with minimal effort, providing steady growth without constant monitoring.

✗ Myth 5: High Returns Are Guaranteed If You Invest in the Right Thing

In the investment world, the saying "if it sounds too good to be true, it probably is" holds significant weight.

Scammers and speculative hype often lure people with promises of guaranteed high returns. We've seen this time and again — whether it was the dot-com bubble of the early 2000s, the real estate crash of 2008, or the cryptocurrency mania of 2017. While some investors made fortunes, many others suffered massive losses because they chased unsustainable gains without understanding the risks.

The reality is that no investment is risk-free. Smart investors focus on long-term value rather than quick wins. They conduct thorough research, assess market conditions, and make calculated decisions instead of chasing fads.

Building a Strong Financial Base

Investing is often glamorised as the key to wealth, but before you start picking stocks or diving into real estate, there's a crucial first step: **ensuring you have a solid financial foundation.**

Investing without stability is like building a house on quicksand. It might stand for a while, but any financial setback can send everything tumbling down. That's why smart investors begin with three key pillars:

- having an emergency fund,
- managing debt wisely, and
- adopting a budget that aligns with long-term wealth creation.

Let's break it down.

Do You Need an Emergency Fund Before Investing?

The short answer? Yes. The longer answer? Absolutely, unless you enjoy the stress of liquidating investments at the worst possible time.

An emergency fund acts as a financial cushion, protecting you from life's unexpected curveballs – things like car repairs, job loss, urgent travel, or even a sudden market downturn. Without it, you might be forced to sell your investments at a loss just to cover everyday expenses.

- **How Much Should You Save?**

Conventional wisdom suggests setting aside three to six months' worth of living expenses in a highly liquid, easily accessible account — think high-yield savings accounts or money market funds. But the right amount depends on your personal circumstances:

Stable income and low expenses? Three months' worth may suffice.

Self-employed or working in an unstable industry? Six months or more may be better.

Multiple income streams? You might get by with a smaller fund, though caution never hurts.

- **The Investment Opportunity Cost Myth**

Some argue that money sitting in a savings account isn't "working" for you. While it's true that emergency funds don't generate high returns, their value lies in liquidity, not profit. The ability to cover an emergency without touching your investments protects long-term growth and keeps your financial strategy intact.

In 2020, during the height of pandemic uncertainty, many investors panicked and sold stocks at a loss to cover short-term needs. Those who had an emergency fund stayed invested and rode the market recovery to significant gains. That's the power of financial preparedness.

Managing Debt:
A Prerequisite for Success

Debt can be a silent wealth killer or a strategic tool, depending on how it's managed. Before committing to investing, it's crucial to differentiate between good debt and bad debt and ensure you aren't paying more in interest than you're likely to earn in returns.

- **Good Debt vs. Bad Debt**

Good Debt: Low-interest, potentially wealth-building liabilities like a mortgage, student loans, or business loans.

Bad Debt: High-interest, depreciating liabilities like credit card balances, payday loans, or unnecessary personal loans.

- **Should You Pay Off Debt Before Investing?**

It depends on the type of debt and its interest rate.

Credit Card Debt (15-25% APR): Pay it off ASAP. There's no investment that can consistently outpace such high-interest rates.

Student Loans (4-7% APR): If rates are on the lower end, investing while making regular payments may be viable.

Mortgage (3-6% APR): Paying extra toward a mortgage may not be the best move if you can invest in assets with higher returns.

A useful rule of thumb: If the interest rate on your debt exceeds the historical average return of the stock market (around 7-10% annually), prioritising debt repayment is the smarter choice.

- **The Snowball vs. Avalanche Method**

If you have multiple debts, consider using the snowball method (paying off the smallest balances first for quick psychological wins) or the avalanche method (targeting the highest-interest debts first to save money long term). Either approach is effective. What matters is consistency and commitment.

By reducing high-interest debt, you free up more of your income for investing while lowering financial risk. There's no point in earning 8% on an investment if you're paying 20% in credit card interest.

Budgeting with an Investor's Perspective

Budgeting isn't just about tracking expenses, it's about ensuring your money is working toward financial freedom. Traditional budgets focus on limiting spending, but an investor's budget emphasises allocating resources effectively to generate long-term wealth.

- **The 50/30/20 Rule With an Investor's Twist**

A common budgeting framework is the 50/30/20 rule:

50% on Needs (housing, groceries, insurance, utilities)
30% on Wants (entertainment, travel, hobbies)
20% on Savings & Investments

However, if financial independence is your goal, consider flipping the script.

30-40% on Investments & Savings
50-60% on Needs & Wants

This shift prioritises asset-building and wealth accumulation while still allowing for an enjoyable lifestyle.

- **Automating Your Investments**

One of the easiest ways to stay consistent is by automating your investments. Setting up recurring contributions to tax-efficient accounts like a Stocks & Shares ISA, a workplace pension, or a Self-Invested Personal Pension (SIPP) ensures you're consistently investing without the temptation to spend the money elsewhere (similar to how US investors use 401(k)s or IRAs).

- **Cutting Costs Without Sacrificing Quality of Life**

Investors don't just budget to reduce spending, they budget to redirect spending toward wealth-building activities. Instead of focusing solely on cutting costs, consider reallocating money from non-essentials toward assets that grow. Some practical shifts include:

Swapping high-end subscriptions for lower-cost alternatives and investing the difference.

Cutting back on takeaways and putting the extra cash to work in the market.

Delaying a luxury purchase in favour of funding an opportunity that generates passive income.

These small, intentional changes compound over time, mirroring the power of compounding in investing.

Setting Clear Investment Goals

Imagine stepping into a car with no destination in mind. You might enjoy the ride for a while, but eventually, you'll wonder where you're going or worse, run out of petrol with nowhere to refuel. Investing without clear goals is much the same. Without a defined purpose, your financial journey becomes a series of random turns, lacking direction or a clear endpoint. Whether you're looking to build wealth over decades or capitalise on short-term opportunities, setting clear investment goals s the foundation of financial success.

Short-Term vs. Long-Term Investing: Understanding the Trade-offs

Before diving into specific investments, you need to distinguish between short term and long-term investing. Both approaches have their place, but they serve different purposes and come with distinct risks and rewards.

- **Short-Term Investing: Quick Wins or Costly Mistakes?**

Short-term investing typically involves a timeframe of a few months to a few years. Investors in this category often look for quick profits, whether through stock trading, options, or even cryptocurrency. The appeal? Potentially high returns in a short period. The downside? Volatility, unpredictability, and the risk of losing substantial capital if the market swings against you.

Consider the example of tech stocks during the pandemic. Companies like Zoom and Tesla saw their share prices skyrocket in 2020, making fortunes for those who bought early and sold at the right time. But by 2022, many of these stocks had tumbled significantly, catching latecomers off guard. Short-term investing demands a keen eye on market trends, a high tolerance for risk, and often, a considerable amount of time spent monitoring the market.

For those who prefer lower risk, short-term investments can also include high-yield savings accounts, money market funds, or short-term bonds. These options won't double your money overnight, but they provide liquidity and stability, ideal for those saving for a down payment on a house, or an upcoming major expense.

- **Long-Term Investing: The Power of Time and Compounding**

Long-term investing, on the other hand, is about patience and strategic wealth-building over many years – even decades. It harnesses the power of compound growth: your investments generate earnings, which are reinvested to produce even more earnings over time.

One of the clearest examples of successful long-term investing is Warren Buffett, often called the Oracle of Omaha. He built his fortune not by chasing trends or trading in and out of the market, but by investing in high-quality companies and holding them for decades — letting time and compounding do the heavy lifting.

For UK investors, a low-cost index fund tracking the FTSE All-Share or a global tracker fund is a solid long-term option. These funds spread your investment across a wide range of established companies, offering built-in diversification. Historically, they've delivered steady growth over time — especially when dividends are reinvested. For example, investing £10,000 and leaving it to grow for 30 or 40 years can result in substantial gains, even with occasional downturns along the way.

The real key? Stay the course. Ignore the noise, resist the urge to time the market, and avoid panic-selling when things get choppy. Long-term investing rewards patience and consistency, not urgency.

Defining Your Risk Tolerance: How Much Uncertainty Can You Handle?

Investing isn't just about numbers, it's about emotions. Understanding your risk tolerance is crucial in crafting an investment strategy that aligns with both your financial goals and psychological comfort level.

- **The Three Types of Investors**

Conservative Investors:
Prefer stability over high returns. They favour bonds, dividend stocks, and other low-volatility assets. If market fluctuations make you lose sleep, this approach might be for you.

Moderate Investors:
Willing to take on some risk for the potential of higher rewards. They balance their portfolios with a mix of stocks, bonds, and real estate, aiming for steady but meaningful growth.

Aggressive Investors:
These investors are comfortable with high volatility and willing to endure short-term losses in pursuit of significant long-term gains. They're often drawn to growth stocks, venture capital, or emerging assets like cryptocurrencies.

Assessing your risk tolerance isn't just about preference; it's about need. If you're young with decades before retirement, you can afford to take more risks. But if you're nearing retirement, capital preservation becomes a higher priority. A good rule of thumb? Invest aggressively when you have time to recover from losses, and shift towards safer investments as you approach major financial milestones.

Aligning Investments with Life Milestones

Investing isn't an isolated activity it's deeply tied to the different stages of your life. Whether you're saving for a home, funding a child's education, or planning for retirement, your investment strategy should evolve alongside your personal and professional goals.

- **Buying a Home: Balancing Growth and Liquidity**

If you're planning to buy a house in the next five years, you don't want to take on excessive risk. Imagine putting your down payment fund in the stock market right before a major crash. You could lose a significant portion of your savings overnight. Instead, opt for low-risk, short-term investments like money market funds, Treasury bonds, or even a high-yield savings account. These options won't generate massive returns, but they'll ensure your capital is preserved and accessible when you need it.

- **Saving for Education: Building a University Fund**

For many parents, funding a child's education is a major financial priority. In the UK, while there's no direct equivalent to the US 529 plan, you can still build a substantial education fund through tax-efficient options like a Junior ISA or a dedicated investment account. By starting early and contributing regularly – ideally through a Stocks & Shares Junior ISA – you give your child's savings the opportunity to grow over time. When invested wisely, this approach can help cover future university costs or give your child a financial head start in adulthood, all while benefiting from tax-free growth and tax-free withdrawals.

- **Retirement Planning: The Long Game**

Retirement planning is the ultimate long-term investment goal. Here, the key is diversification. A well-balanced portfolio should include stocks for growth, bonds for stability, and possibly real estate or annuities for additional income streams.

The advantage of starting early? You give compounding the time it needs to work its magic.

Let's say you start investing £400 a month at age 25 in a low-cost index fund, earning an average annual return of 8%. By the time you reach 65, you could have built a pot worth around £1.39 million. But if you wait until age 35 to start, that figure drops to about £596,000 – less than half.

The bottom line? Time matters more than timing. The earlier you begin, the more your money can grow – even if your monthly contributions stay the same.

Every investment involves some level of risk – but that risk should match your goals, timeline, and emotional comfort zone. Here's how to approach it:

☐ **Know the Basics**

Higher potential returns usually come with higher risk. Low-risk investments often grow more slowly, but are more stable.

☐ **Match Risk to Your Time Horizon**

Investing for retirement in 25 years? You can afford to take more risk.

Saving for a house in 3 years? You'll want something more stable.

☐ Ask Yourself: How Would I Feel If...

My portfolio dropped 20% in a month?

I saw no growth for a year?

Would I sell... or stay the course?

☐ Diversify to Smooth the Ride

Spread your money across different asset classes (shares, bonds, property) so no single event derails your progress.

☐ Remember: Doing Nothing Is Also a Risk

Leaving money in cash might feel safe—but inflation slowly eats it away. Over time, not investing can be more dangerous than investing wisely.

Don't Let These Myths Hold You Back

New investors are often put off by half-truths and outdated ideas. Let's clear a few of them up:

✗ Myth: "You need a lot of money to start investing."

✅ Fact: You can get started with just £25-£50 a month using platforms like Vanguard, Freetrade, or Nutmeg.

✗ Myth: "Investing is the same as gambling."

✅ Fact: Gambling is luck-based. Investing is about long-term ownership of assets that grow in value and produce income.

✗ Myth: "I'll wait for the market to crash – then I'll invest."

✅ Fact: Timing the market is nearly impossible. Time in the market matters more than timing the market.

✗ Myth: "Only experts can invest successfully."

✅ Fact: Most professional investors don't beat the market. Simple index funds often outperform them.

✗ Myth: "I'll lose everything in a crash."

✅ Fact: Markets go up and down – but historically, they've always recovered. Diversification and staying invested are key.

✗ Myth: "It's too late for me to start."

✅ Fact: The best time to start was yesterday. The second-best time is today.

Build Your Foundation First

Before you start investing, it's essential to build a solid financial foundation. Think of it as setting up a safety net that allows you to weather market ups and downs without feeling the pressure to make hasty decisions. Once your foundation is in place, you'll have the confidence to stay the course.

Here's how to build that base:

☐ Emergency Fund
Save 3-6 months of essential living expenses in an easy-access savings account. This protects your investments from being raided in a crisis.

☐ Pay Off High-Interest Debt
Clear credit cards, payday loans, and any other debts with high interest. These are guaranteed to cost you more than any investment can earn.

☐ Understand Good vs Bad Debt
Not all debt is evil—but it must be managed. A low-interest mortgage on a home may be "good debt." But borrowing to invest? That's risky ground.

☐ Master Your Budget
Track what's coming in and going out. Know your "spend number." Free up some cash to invest – even £50 a month is a great start.

☐ Create Margin
Give yourself breathing space. Living pay cheque to pay cheque makes it hard to stay invested when life throws curveballs.

PART TWO

Navigating the Investment Landscape

Investing isn't just about picking a stock and hoping it skyrockets overnight. It's about understanding the vast ecosystem of opportunities available to you, each with its own risk-reward balance, economic influences, and potential for long-term growth. Whether you're just dipping your toes into the market or refining an existing strategy, grasping the nuances of various investment vehicles can help you make informed, confident decisions.

Breaking Down Investment Options

The world of investing can feel overwhelming, but at its core, it's about channelling capital into assets that generate returns over time. Stocks, bonds, real estate, cryptocurrencies, and alternative investments all serve different roles in wealth-building, and each comes with unique considerations. The key is understanding how these vehicles function and determining which aligns with your goals, risk tolerance, and time horizon.

Stocks, Bonds, and Beyond: What Are Your Choices?

- **Stocks: Ownership in Growth**

When you buy a stock, you're purchasing a share of a company, effectively becoming a part-owner. This ownership entitles you to a slice of the company's profits (via dividends) and the potential for capital appreciation as the company grows. Historically, stocks have delivered higher long-term returns compared to other asset classes, but they also come with higher volatility.

For instance, a company like Apple saw its stock rise over 300% between 2015 and 2023, rewarding long-term investors handsomely. However, it's not always smooth sailing. The stock market is influenced by economic cycles, interest rates, and investor sentiment, which can cause sharp swings. The 2020 pandemic-induced market crash saw the S&P 500 plummet nearly 35% in just a few weeks before rebounding, demonstrating both the risks and resilience of equities.

Bonds: Stability in Volatile Times

Bonds, on the other hand, offer a more predictable income stream. Essentially, a bond is a loan you provide to a government or corporation in exchange for regular interest payments and the return of your initial investment at maturity. In the UK, government bonds – known as gilts – are considered among the safest investments, as they are backed by the UK government (similar to US Treasury bonds in the United States).

Corporate bonds offer higher yields but carry varying levels of risk depending on the issuer's financial health. High-yield bonds (or "junk bonds") provide lucrative returns but come with a greater chance of default. During the 2008 financial crisis, bondholders of companies like Lehman Brothers faced devastating losses, underscoring the importance of risk assessment in fixed-income investing.

Real Estate, Crypto, and Alternative Investments: Worth the Hype?

- **Real Estate: Tangible Wealth-Building**

Real estate has long been a cornerstone of wealth accumulation. From rental properties to commercial spaces, investing in physical assets offers cash flow, tax benefits, and the potential for long-term appreciation.

Take the UK property market in the early 2020s, for example. Ultra-low interest rates drove demand, pushing property values to new highs in areas like London, Manchester, and Bristol. However, as the Bank of England began raising rates sharply in 2022 and 2023 to curb inflation, mortgage affordability declined, cooling the housing market and highlighting real estate's sensitivity to economic conditions.

For investors who want property exposure without the burden of being a landlord, Real Estate Investment Trusts (REITs) listed on the London Stock Exchange provide access to income-generating property portfolios. They offer a hands-off approach to real estate investing, often with regular dividends and liquidity.

- **Cryptocurrency: The High-Risk, High-Reward Frontier**

Cryptocurrency has been one of the most polarising investment classes in recent years. Bitcoin, once dismissed as a fringe experiment, surged from under $1,000 in 2017 to over $60,000 in 2021 before experiencing wild swings. Crypto's appeal lies in decentralisation, potential protection against inflation, and explosive growth—but it remains highly speculative, volatile, and largely unregulated.

The 2022 collapse of FTX, a major crypto exchange, wiped out billions in investor funds and served as a cautionary tale. Still, institutional investors – including major asset managers – are exploring crypto-backed investment products, suggesting that crypto is likely to remain part of the financial landscape. For UK investors, platforms such as eToro and Coinbase make crypto accessible, but due diligence, risk awareness, and diversification are absolutely essential.

Alternative Investments: Diversification Beyond the Norm

Alternative investments can provide diversification benefits that traditional stocks and bonds may not offer. These include hedge funds, commodities, private equity, and even collectibles like fine art, wine, and classic cars.

Assets such as gold have long served as a safe haven during times of high inflation or economic uncertainty. When equity markets falter, gold prices often rise, making it attractive for more risk-conscious investors. Some UK investors also explore alternative platforms offering access to peer-to-peer lending, venture capital, or startup crowdfunding (through providers like Seedrs or Crowdcube).

ETFs vs. Mutual Funds: What's Right for You?

- **Exchange-Traded Funds (ETFs): Flexibility and Low Costs**

ETFs have become increasingly popular in the UK for their low fees, transparency, and ease of trading. They allow you to invest in a wide range of companies or sectors through one product, and can be bought and sold throughout the trading day – just like shares.

For example, the iShares Core FTSE 100 ETF gives exposure to 100 of the UK's largest companies, while the Vanguard FTSE All-World ETF offers global diversification. Thematic ETFs focusing on clean energy, technology, or ESG investing are also growing in popularity among UK investors.

- **Mutual Funds: Managed for the Long Haul**

In the UK, mutual funds are more commonly referred to as unit trusts or Open-Ended Investment Companies (OEICs). These funds pool investors' money to create diversified portfolios, usually managed by professional fund managers.

Actively managed funds can outperform the market—but often at the cost of higher fees and underperformance risk. While they can suit hands-off investors, the combination of higher charges and less flexibility means many modern investors now prefer ETFs.

How the Market Works

The stock market might seem like a chaotic, unpredictable beast, but beneath the surface, it follows patterns shaped by economic forces, investor psychology, and financial fundamentals. Understanding these underlying principles isn't just for economists or Wall Street insiders, it's essential for anyone looking to navigate the world of investing with confidence. Let's break down some of the most important aspects of market behaviour: bull and bear markets, the impact of interest rates and inflation, and the role of economic cycles in smart investing.

Understanding Bull and Bear Markets

At its core, the market moves in cycles of optimism and pessimism, commonly referred to as bull and bear markets. A bull market is characterised by rising stock prices, growing investor confidence, and an overall positive economic outlook. Investors rush to buy, companies expand, and wealth creation feels almost effortless. Take the period from 2009 to early 2020 – a historic bull market fuelled by technological innovation, low interest rates, and steady economic growth. Investors who stayed in the game reaped significant rewards.

On the flip side, a bear market signals a period of decline, where stock prices fall by 20% or more from recent highs. Fear sets in, and many investors sell off their holdings, while economic indicators often point to a potential recession. The

2008 financial crisis, which was triggered by the collapse of the housing market and a banking crisis, wiped out trillions in wealth. However, those who remained patient and invested in undervalued assets during the downturn saw significant gains when the market eventually recovered.

The key takeaway? Bull and bear markets are natural parts of the economic cycle. Investors who recognise these trends and, more importantly, remain disciplined through them position themselves for long-term success. Instead of reacting emotionally to market fluctuations, successful investors develop strategies that allow them to capitalise on both upswings and downturns.

How Interest Rates and Inflation Shape Investing Strategies

Interest rates and inflation act as powerful levers that influence nearly every aspect of investing. When the Bank of England adjusts the base rate (similar to the Federal Reserve adjusting rates in the US), it sends ripples across the economy, affecting everything from mortgage rates and savings returns to stock valuations.

- **Interest Rates: The Cost of Money**

When interest rates are low, borrowing is cheap, businesses expand, and consumers spend more. This environment tends to push stock prices higher, as corporate profits rise and economic activity flourishes. For example, in the wake of the COVID-19 pandemic, central banks slashed interest rates to near zero, fuelling an explosive recovery in stock prices, particularly in growth sectors like technology.

However, when interest rates rise, borrowing becomes more expensive, consumer spending slows, and corporate growth stalls. This often leads to declining stock prices, especially in sectors that rely heavily on debt financing, like real estate and high-growth tech startups. Investors typically shift toward more conservative assets, such as bonds, which become more attractive as yields rise.

- **Inflation: The Erosion of Purchasing Power**

Inflation — where the price of goods and services rises over time — plays a crucial role in investment decisions. Moderate inflation (typically around 2%) is considered healthy, as it signals a growing economy. However, when inflation surges unexpectedly, as it did in the UK between 2021 and 2023 when rates peaked above 11%, it erodes purchasing power and unnerves investors, often triggering shifts in strategy toward more inflation-resistant assets.

Stocks can offer a hedge against inflation, but not all sectors perform equally. Commodities (like gold and oil), real estate, and companies with strong pricing power tend to do well in inflationary environments. Conversely, fixed-income investments, such as bonds, suffer as their real returns shrink. Understanding how inflation and interest rates interact helps investors adjust their portfolios accordingly whether it means shifting into inflation-resistant assets or rebalancing toward higher-yield opportunities.

The Role of Economic Cycles in Smart Investing

The economy moves through four broad cycles: expansion, peak, contraction, and trough, each of which influences investment strategies differently.

- **Expansion: The Growth Phase**

During expansion, businesses thrive, unemployment is low, and consumer confidence is high. This phase, typically marked by rising stock prices, is when investors feel most optimistic. Growth stocks, especially in sectors like technology and consumer discretionary, tend to outperform during market upswings. This can be a good time to ride the momentum – but it's also important to stay mindful of overvalued assets.

- **Peak: The Warning Sign**

At the peak of the cycle, economic growth starts to slow, inflation creeps up, and central banks may raise interest rates to prevent overheating. Stock valuations often become stretched, and speculative bubbles can form. A classic example is the dot-com bubble of the late 1990s, when excessive optimism in tech stocks led to unsustainable valuations. Savvy investors recognise the warning signs –

high valuations, slowing earnings growth – and begin rebalancing toward defensive sectors like utilities, healthcare, and consumer staples.

- **Contraction: The Downturn**

In the contraction phase, the economy slows, layoffs increase, and corporate earnings decline. The market turns bearish, and fear takes hold. This is when investors face their biggest test: do they panic and sell, or do they see opportunities in undervalued assets? Historically, the best investment opportunities arise during downturns. Investors who picked up high-quality stocks during the 2008-2009 recession or the COVID-19 crash in early 2020 saw enormous gains in the following years.

- **Trough: The Turning Point**

At the trough, the economy stabilises, interest rates often decline, and early signs of recovery emerge. This is the moment when the most significant wealth-building opportunities arise. Investors who recognise the shift can position themselves for the next expansion by loading up on growth-oriented assets before the broader market catches on.

The Psychology of Investing

Investing isn't just about numbers, charts, or financial models it's a deeply psychological game. The ability to manage emotions, stay disciplined, and avoid impulsive decisions often separates successful investors from those who consistently lose money. The stock market is a battleground where fear and greed clash, where human psychology drives bubbles, crashes, and once-in-a-lifetime opportunities. Understanding how these emotions influence your decisions is crucial if you want to build long-term wealth and navigate market volatility with confidence.

Fear, Greed, and Market Volatility

Picture this: The stock market is soaring, and everyone you know is talking about their latest investments. News headlines are filled with success stories of ordinary people doubling or even tripling their money overnight. Greed takes over. You feel like you're missing out, so you jump in, convinced that this upward momentum will never end. Then, almost without warning, the market crashes. Panic sets in.

Your portfolio is bleeding, and every instinct tells you to sell before you lose everything.

This cycle of euphoria and despair has repeated itself throughout history. In the late 1990s, investors rushed into tech stocks during the dot-com boom, driven by the belief that the internet would change everything (which it did, but not every company survived). When the bubble burst, many lost fortunes. The same story unfolded in 2008 with the housing market crash, and again in 2021, when speculative assets like cryptocurrencies and meme stocks skyrocketed before plunging.

Market volatility is inevitable, but the way investors react to it determines their success. Fear makes people sell at the worst possible time, locking in losses. Greed blinds them to risk, leading them to overextend themselves when prices are high. Both emotions create the illusion that investing is more unpredictable than it actually is. The truth is, markets move in cycles, and long-term success depends on recognising these emotional traps and resisting knee-jerk reactions.

Avoiding Common Pitfalls Like FOMO and Panic Selling

One of the most dangerous psychological traps in investing is FOMO – Fear of Missing Out. It's what drives people to buy assets at their peak, convinced that if they don't act now, they'll miss a once-in-a-lifetime opportunity. We saw this in 2020 and 2021 when retail investors poured into speculative stocks like GameStop and AMC, driven by social media hype rather than sound financial analysis. Some made money, but many bought at the top and watched their investments crumble.

FOMO is fuelled by social proof. When everyone around you is making money, it's hard to stay on the sidelines. But a fundamental rule of investing is that opportunities are always present you just need to know where to look. Instead of chasing the latest trend, focus on your long-term strategy and stick to investments that align with your goals.

At the other end of the spectrum is panic selling – the urge to liquidate everything when the market takes a downturn. This is often triggered by media-driven hysteria, exaggerated worst-case scenarios, or simply watching your portfolio shrink. In 2008, many investors sold at the bottom, only to miss the massive recovery that followed. Similarly, in March 2020, when COVID-19 sent markets into a tailspin, those who sold in fear missed out on one of the fastest market rebounds in history.

The best way to avoid these emotional pitfalls? Have a plan. Set clear investment goals, decide in advance how much risk you're willing to tolerate, and remind yourself that downturns are temporary. If your investments are fundamentally sound, volatility is an opportunity, not a death sentence.

Emotional Discipline: The Key to Long-Term Wealth

Warren Buffett famously said, "The stock market is a device for transferring money from the impatient to the patient." This wisdom highlights one of the most critical traits of successful investors: emotional discipline.

What does emotional discipline look like in practice?

- **Sticking to a Strategy**

Successful investors don't let emotions dictate their actions. Instead, they follow a disciplined approach whether it's value investing, index fund investing, or another proven strategy. They trust their research and stay the course, even when markets get turbulent.

- **Reframing Volatility as Opportunity**

Instead of viewing market drops as threats, disciplined investors see them as opportunities. When high-quality stocks go on sale, they buy more. This mindset shift from fear to strategic action can make a huge difference in long-term wealth accumulation.

- **Setting Rules to Counteract Emotional Bias**

One effective strategy is Pound-Cost averaging, which involves investing a fixed amount at regular intervals, regardless of market conditions. This removes the temptation to time the market and reduces the impact of short-term volatility. Another approach is using stop-loss orders or rebalancing your portfolio periodically to maintain your desired level of risk.

- **Tuning Out the Noise**

The financial media thrive on sensationalism. Headlines scream "Market Meltdown!" or "Greatest Buying Opportunity Ever!" both designed to provoke emotional reactions. The best investors learn to tune out the noise and focus on long-term fundamentals rather than short-term speculation.

- **Adopting a Long-Term Perspective**

Investing isn't about making a quick buck it's about building wealth over time. The stock market has historically trended upward despite recessons, political turmoi, and financial crises. Those who stay invested and continue to make smart, calculated moves tend to come out ahead.

Choosing the Right Investment Type: What to Consider

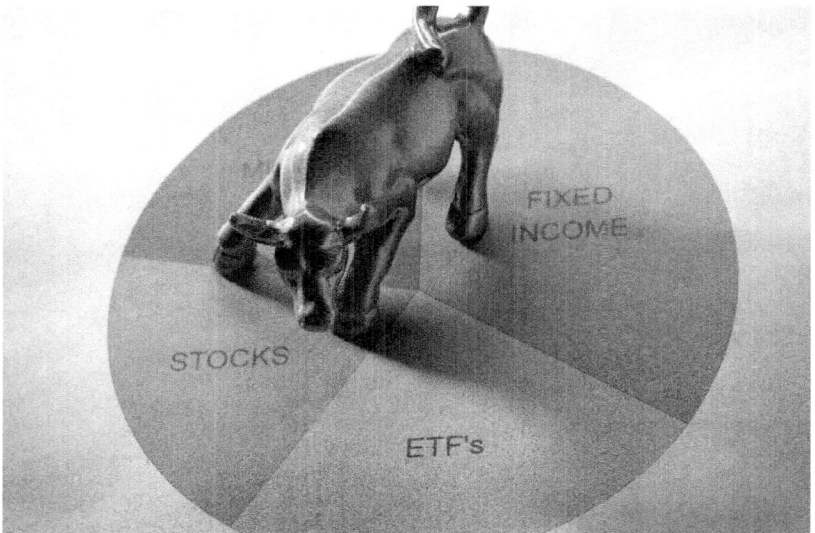

When deciding where to put your money, keep these pointers in mind:

Stocks

✓ High potential returns

✓ Greater volatility

✓ Suitable for long-term growth

Bonds

✓ More stable income

✓ Lower risk than stocks

✓ Useful for diversification and capital preservation

Real Estate

✓ Tangible asset

✓ Potential rental income + long-term appreciation

✓ Illiquid and sensitive to economic conditions

Cryptocurrency

✓ High risk, high reward

✓ Extreme volatility

✓ Only invest what you can afford to lose

Alternative Investments

✓ Includes gold, private equity, collectibles

✓ Adds diversification

✓ Requires deeper research and risk awareness

ETFs vs Unit Trusts/OEICs

✓ ETFs: lower costs, tradable like shares

✓ Unit Trusts/OEICs: professional management, less flexibility

Market Cycles & Economic Conditions

✓ Recognise bull vs bear markets

✓ Understand the 4 economic phases (expansion, peak, contraction, trough)

✓ Stay consistent and long-term focused

PART THREE

CRAFTING YOUR STRATEGY

So, you're ready to start investing, but the sheer number of options, strategies, and market dynamics feels overwhelming. Where do you begin? What makes a portfolio solid, adaptable, and capable of weathering economic storms? The key is a well-thought-out strategy tailored to your risk tolerance, financial goals, and time horizon. Let's break down the fundamentals of constructing a beginner-friendly investment portfolio.

The Importance of Diversification

Imagine walking a tightrope. If you have a balancing pole, your movements are more stable and controlled. Diversification in investing works much the same way it spreads your risk across different assets so that if one falters, others can help keep your portfolio steady.

Diversification isn't just about holding multiple stocks; it's about balancing across asset classes: stocks, bonds, real estate, commodities, and even alternative investments like REITs or ETFs. Why? Because different assets react differently to market conditions. When stocks dip due to economic uncertainty, bonds often hold steady or even rise. If inflation spikes, commodities like gold might become more attractive.

Take the 2008 financial crisis as an example. Investors with a stock-heavy portfolio saw catastrophic losses, while those who had allocated part of their assets to bonds and gold experienced softer blows. The lesson? Avoid putting all your eggs in one basket.

For beginners, a simple way to diversify is by investing in broad-market index funds or ETFs, which give you exposure to hundreds of companies at once. A classic example is the S&P 500 ETF (SPY), which tracks 500 of the largest US companies, instantly giving you a slice of multiple industries.

Another practical method is the 60/40 portfolio rule a mix of 60% equities and 40% bonds, which historically offers a balance of growth and stability. Of course, your ideal mix will depend on your age, risk tolerance, and financial goals.

Passive vs. Active Investing: Which Suits You?

One of the most debated topics in investing is whether to take a hands-off approach (passive investing) or try to beat the market through active investing. Both strategies have their merits, and understanding their differences can help you align with what fits your personality and goals.

- **Passive Investing: The Long Game**

Passive investing is like planting a tree – you nurture it, give it time, and let it grow naturally. It involves investing in index funds or ETFs that track the market, requiring minimal effort beyond the initial selection. Warren Buffett, one of the greatest investors of all time, has repeatedly advised the average investor to put their money into a low-cost S&P 500 index fund and leave it for decades. Why? Because history shows that the market, despite short-term volatility, trends upward over time.

- **Passive investing is perfect for those who:**
  ✓ Prefer a low-maintenance, low-cost approach.
  ✓ Believe in the long-term growth of the market rather than short-term speculation.
  ✓ Want to avoid frequent buying and selling, which can erode returns due to fees and taxes.

- **Active Investing: The Hands-On Approach**

Active investing, on the other hand, is like being a professional athlete it requires training, research, and constant adaptability. It involves picking individual stocks, analysing financial statements, monitoring economic trends, and frequently adjusting positions.

Active investors aim to outperform the market, but here's the reality: most fail to do so consistently. Studies show that over 85% of actively managed funds underperform the S&P 500 over the long run. However, that doesn't mean active investing is useless, it can work for those who are willing to dedicate time to deep research and strategy.

- **Active investing suits those who:**
  ✓ Enjoy researching companies, financial reports, and market trends.
  ✓ Are comfortable with higher risk and potential volatility.
  ✓ Have the discipline to stick to a strategy without emotional decision-making.

For most beginners, a hybrid approach works best starting with passive index funds and gradually exploring active investing as you gain confidence and knowledge.

Pound-Cost Averaging: A Simple Yet Powerful Strategy

If there's one strategy that both passive and active investors can benefit from, it's Pound-Cost Averaging (PCA). It's simple, effective, and helps eliminate the stress of market timing.

PCA involves investing a fixed amount of money at regular intervals whether the market is up or down. Instead of dumping a lump sum into the market at once (which could backfire if prices plummet shortly after), PCA smooths out volatility over time.

- **Why PCA Works**
  - ✓ It Reduces the Impact of Market Fluctuations – Since you're buying at different price points, you naturally average out the cost per share over time.
  - ✓ It Eliminates Emotional Investing – Many investors panic and sell when the market drops or rush to buy when prices skyrocket. PCA removes the pressure of guessing when to invest.
  - ✓ It Encourages Discipline – By automating investments, you stick to a plan and consistently build wealth.

- **Real-World Example: Investing in the S&P 500**

Let's say you decide to invest £500 per month into an S&P 500 index fund. Some months, the market will be high, and you'll buy fewer shares; other months, the market will dip, and you'll buy more shares at a discount. Over decades, this strategy has historically led to substantial returns.

For example, someone who started investing in the S&P 500 in 2000 including during the 2008 crash using PCA would have still seen strong long-term gains, despite short-term dips.

- **When PCA Might Not Be Ideal**

If you have a large lump sum, investing all at once may yield better results (historically, lump-sum investing outperforms PCA about 70% of the time, but with higher short-term risk).

In a consistently declining market, PCA won't protect you from long-term losses, though it still cushions the impact.

For most beginners, though, PCA is a fantastic entry strategy. It removes complexity, lowers stress, and ensures you're consistently putting money to work.

Before you move from building your strategy to picking specific investments, there's one final—and often overlooked—piece of the puzzle to address: Tax!

How and where you hold your investments can make a huge difference to your overall returns. Even the best-performing portfolio can under-deliver if it's taxed inefficiently. Fortunately, the UK offers several tax-efficient wrappers that can help protect your gains and boost your long-term wealth.

Tax and Your Investments: What You Need to Know

Tax might not be the most exciting part of investing—but it's one of the most important. Understanding how your investments are taxed in the UK can help you make smarter decisions and keep more of your money working for you.

The Taxes Investors Face

If you invest outside of a tax-efficient account (like a Stocks & Shares ISA or a SIPP), you may have to pay the following:

- **Capital Gains Tax (CGT):**

This applies when you sell an investment at a profit.

You can currently earn up to £1,000 in capital gains each tax year tax-free. Anything above that is taxed at 10% (basic-rate taxpayers) or 20% (higher-rate taxpayers).

- **Dividend Tax:**

If you receive dividend payments (typically from shares or equity funds), the first £500 is tax-free.

Above that, dividends are taxed at 8.75%, 33.75%, or 39.35%, depending on your income bracket.

- **Income Tax:**

Interest from bonds or savings accounts may count as income. Some of it might be covered by your Personal Savings Allowance (£1,000 for basic-rate taxpayers), but the rest could be taxed as ordinary income.

Use Tax-Efficient Accounts

You can avoid most of this complexity by using ISA and SIPP accounts, which offer powerful tax benefits:

Stocks & Shares ISA:

- No tax on capital gains
- No tax on dividends

- No tax on interest

- Withdraw anytime, tax-free

- You can invest up to £20,000 per year

SIPP (Self-Invested Personal Pension):

- No tax on gains, dividends, or interest

- Contributions benefit from tax relief (the government tops up your contributions)

- You can start withdrawing from age 55 (rising to 57 by 2028), with 25% tax-free, and the rest taxed as income

Tax-Efficient Strategy Tip

If you're investing for the long term, prioritise filling your ISA allowance first, then consider a SIPP for retirement. Taxable general investment acccounts can be useful too—but be aware of the limits and plan your withdrawals carefully.

Making Smart Decisions in Any Market

Investing isn't just about picking stocks and hoping for the best it's about making informed, strategic decisions that keep your portfolio growing even when markets are unpredictable. Whether the economy is soaring or stalling, smart investors know how to navigate uncertainty with confidence. That's what separates those who build lasting wealth from those who panic and lose out.

When to Buy, Hold, or Sell

There's no single formula for timing the market, but there are principles that can help guide your decisions. The key? Thinking long-term while staying flexible enough to adapt when needed.

Buying at the right time isn't about chasing hype it's about recognising value. Legendary investors like Warren Buffett emphasise the importance of buying great companies at reasonable prices rather than chasing the latest trend. When a stock is trading below its intrinsic value due to short-term fears or market fluctuations, that's often an opportunity. Take the 2020 market crash, for example. While many panicked, those who saw it as a buying opportunity reaped significant rewards when the market rebounded.

Holding, despite being the least exciting action, is often the most powerful. Remember, time in the market beats timing the market. Investors who hold strong companies through temporary downturns tend to outperform those who jump in and out of positions. The classic example? Amazon. Many investors sold during its early struggles, missing out on its meteoric rise. Patience often pays off, especially for companies with strong fundamentals.

Selling is trickier. Too often, investors sell either out of fear or overconfidence. A stock losing value doesn't automatically mean it's a bad investment – sometimes, markets are just irrational in the short term. The best time to sell is when a company's fundamentals have changed for the worse, not just because the price has dipped. If a company is losing market share, drowning in unsustainable debt, or its industry is in decline, then it may be time to move on. On the flip side, taking profits when a stock is significantly overvalued can also be a smart move.

Reading Financial Statements Without Getting Overwhelmed

Financial statements may seem intimidating, but they tell a story — one of a company's health, growth potential, and risk factors. The trick is knowing what matters most.

Start with the income statement, which shows revenue, expenses, and profitability. The top line (revenue) tells you how much money is coming in, while the bottom line (net profit) shows what's left after expenses. A company with growing revenue but shrinking profits could signal trouble, while steady profit margins suggest operational efficiency.

The balance sheet is your snapshot of financial stability. Look at assets versus liabilities. A company with too much debt may struggle when interest rates rise, while a healthy cash reserve gives it flexibility in tough times. Apple, for example, maintains a massive cash reserve, allowing it to weather economic downturns and seize new opportunities.

Finally, the cash flow statement tells you where money is actually going. Even a profitable company can fail if it lacks cash flow. Positive operating cash flow shows a business is generating money from its core operations, while negative cash flow can be a red flag unless it's due to heavy investment in future growth.

Rather than getting lost in numbers, focus on trends. Is revenue growing? Are debts manageable? Does cash flow support future expansion? These insights will tell you far more than any single data point.

Understanding Market Trends and Indicators

The market isn't random it moves in cycles, influenced by economic factors, investor sentiment, and external events. Knowing what drives these shifts helps investors stay ahead rather than react in panic.

Economic indicators provide valuable clues. Interest rates, inflation, and employment data all shape market behaviour. When interest rates rise, borrowing costs increase, often slowing growth in sectors like real estate and tech. On the other hand, falling interest rates can spark economic expansion and higher stock prices.

Then there's market sentiment, which can push stocks to irrational highs or devastating lows. The dot-com bubble of the late 1990s saw sky-high valuations based on speculation rather than actual earnings. Understanding investor psychology helps you avoid overpaying during euphoria or selling too soon during downturns.

Technical analysis, though often associated with day traders, can be useful even for long-term investors. Support and resistance levels, moving averages, and momentum indicators help identify when stocks are overbought or oversold. For example, when a stock repeatedly bounces off a certain price, that level becomes a key indicator for future movements.

The best investors blend fundamental analysis with an awareness of market trends. They don't chase short-term gains but remain adaptable, recognising when shifts in the economy or industry require a strategy adjustment.

Leveraging Technology and Resources in Investing

In today's digital age, the world of investing has transformed dramatically. Gone are the days of calling a broker or poring over financial newspapers for the latest market news. Technology has not only democratised investing but also made it more efficient, accessible, and data-driven. Whether you're just starting out or are a seasoned investor seeking advanced strategies, using the right tools can help you make better decisions and stay ahead of market trends.

Investment Apps and Robo-Advisors: Do They Work?

For many, investing can feel intimidating – too complex, too risky, and too time-consuming. That's where investment apps and robo-advisers come in, making it easier than ever to get started with minimal effort. But do they really work?

Investment apps like Freetrade, eToro, and Trading 212 have transformed retail investing in the UK by eliminating commissions and offering user-friendly interfaces that let investors buy and sell stocks, ETFs, and even cryptocurrency with just a few taps. Meanwhile, UK-based robo-advisers such as Nutmeg, Moneyfarm, and Wealthify provide algorithm-driven portfolio management tailored to individual risk tolerance and financial goals. These platforms use technology to automate investing, reinvest dividends, and optimise asset allocation – all at a fraction of the cost of traditional financial advisers.

For passive investors, robo-advisers can be a game-changer. They automate the investing process, reducing the risk of emotional decision-making and ensuring long-term consistency. However, they're not without limitations. A robo-advisor won't provide the personalised insights or strategic planning that a human financial advisor can offer, making them better suited for those with simpler financial needs rather than high-net-worth individuals seeking complex wealth management.

On the other hand, DIY investment apps give individuals the freedom to make their own investment choices – but with that freedom comes responsibility. The ease and immediacy of trading can sometimes lead to impulsive decisions, especially during periods of market volatility.

A notable example was the 2021 GameStop short squeeze, where retail investors – coordinating through Reddit's WallStreetBets forum and trading on apps like Robinhood – drove up the stock price dramatically. While some early investors made large gains, many who bought in at the peak suffered steep losses. The event made global headlines, highlighting both the growing influence of retail investors and the risks of emotionally driven or speculative trading, particularly when fuelled by social media hype.

In the UK, similar trading activity occurred on platforms like Freetrade and Trading 212, where users could access US-listed stocks and participate in global market trends with just a few taps. While technology has made investing more accessible than ever, it has also made discipline and long-term thinking more important than ever.

So, do these tools work? The answer depends on the investor. For those who value automation, robo-advisers offer a disciplined approach to wealth building. For hands-on investors, apps provide flexibility but require financial literacy and self-control. The best approach may be a combination of both – using robo-advisers for long-term investments while leveraging apps for strategic, self-directed trades.

How to Research Stocks and Funds Like a Pro

Investing isn't just about picking stocks based on gut feeling or the latest news. Successful investors approach the market with research-backed decisions. But with an overwhelming amount of information available, how do you sift through the noise?

Start with the fundamentals. Whether you're analysing individual stocks or ETFs, key financial metrics can offer valuable insight into a company's health and growth potential. Websites such as Yahoo Finance, Morningstar, and Hargreaves Lansdown, as well as tools like Trustnet or Simply Wall St, provide easy access to earnings reports, balance sheets, and valuation ratios such as the P/E (Price-to-Earnings) ratio, EPS (Earnings Per Share), and ROE (Return on Equity). These figures can help you assess whether a stock appears undervalued, overvalued, or fairly priced – an essential step before making an informed investment decision.

Beyond numbers, understanding a company's business model, competitive advantage, and industry trends is essential. Take Tesla, for example. While its P/E ratio often appears sky-high compared to traditional automakers, investors consider its dominance in the electric vehicle (EV) market, innovation in battery technology, and potential expansion into autonomous driving as factors justifying its valuation. Analysing not just financials but also long-term growth catalysts can separate an average investor from a great one.

When considering ETFs or managed funds (such as unit trusts or OEICs), it's important to evaluate factors like expense ratios, diversification, and historical performance. Index-tracking funds – such as the Vanguard FTSE All-World ETF or iShares Core FTSE 100 ETF – have consistently delivered solid returns with low fees, making them a popular choice for long-term UK investors. Some investors still opt for US-focused funds like Vanguard's VOO (which tracks the S&P 500) for global diversification.

A fund's composition – whether it focuses on growth stocks, value stocks, emerging markets, or specific sectors–should match your investment goals and risk tolerance.

Technical analysis can also be useful, especially for short-term traders looking to time their entries and exits based on price trends and market signals, though it's less essential for long-term, passive strategies. Platforms like Trading View and Thinkor Swim provide charting tools to analyse price patterns, moving averages, and market trends. However, while technical indicators can be helpful, they should complement not replace fundamental research.

Lastly, investor sentiment matters. Market psychology often drives stock movements beyond logic. Keeping an eye on news, earnings calls, and even social media chatter can help you spot shifts in mood that might not yet be reflected in the numbers.

When fear takes hold of the market, even great companies can become undervalued. And when hype takes over, prices can surge far beyond their true worth. Learning to stay calm — and act rationally when others don't — is one of the most valuable skills you can develop as an investor.

Learning from the Best: Books, Podcasts, and Experts to Follow

One of the fastest ways to accelerate your investing knowledge is by learning from those who've mastered the game. Fortunately, today's digital world offers a wealth of resources from classic books to expert-led podcasts that can provide invaluable insights.

If you're new to investing, books like "The Intelligent Investor" by Benjamin Graham and "Common Stocks and Uncommon Profits" by Philip Fisher lay the foundation for understanding value investing and growth strategies. For those interested in behavioural finance, "Thinking, Fast and Slow" by Daniel Kahneman explores the psychology behind financial decision-making and market irrationality. Meanwhile, "One

Up on Wall Street" by Peter Lynch teaches how everyday investors can spot winning stocks by observing trends in daily life.

Podcasts have also become an essential tool for staying updated on market trends. "The Invest Like the Best" podcast by Patrick O'Shaughnessy offers deep dives into investment strategies, while "The Motley Fool Money" podcast breaks down financial news in an engaging and accessible way. For a mix of entertainment and education, "Animal Spirits" by Michael Batnick and Ben Carlson provides fresh perspectives on market behaviour and financial planning.

Beyond books and podcasts, following industry leaders on Twitter and LinkedIn can provide real-time insights. Investors like Warren Buffett, Ray Dalio, and Cathie Wood frequently share their perspectives on economic shifts, stock movements, and macro trends. Hedge fund managers like Bill Ackman or venture capitalists like Chamath Palihapitiya often provide bold predictions that, while sometimes controversial, can challenge conventional thinking and spark new ideas.

Ultimately, the best investors never stop learning. Markets evolve, economic conditions shift, and new opportunities emerge constantly. By leveraging the right tools, staying informed, and refining your strategy over time, you can navigate the world of investing with confidence and purpose.

Let's Recap:

- ✓ Diversification is Key – Spreading investments across asset classes reduces risk and enhances stability.
- ✓ Passive vs. Active Investing – Passive investing is low-cost and long-term, while active investing requires time and research.
- ✓ Pound-Cost Averaging (PCA) – Helps manage market volatility by investing fixed amounts consistently over time.
- ✓ Smart Market Decisions – Avoid emotional investing; focus on fundamentals and long-term growth.
- ✓ Financial Statements Matter – Understanding company financials helps assess investment potential.
- ✓ Market Trends & Indicators – Economic conditions and technical signals guide better investment choices.

PART FOUR

The Power of Compound Growth

The difference between those who build wealth and those who simply earn a pay cheque often comes down to one fundamental concept: compound growth. It's not about how much you make it's about how effectively you allow your money to work for you. This principle is at the heart of long-term investing, and when understood and applied correctly, it can be the most powerful wealth-building tool at your disposal.

Real Stories of Everyday Investors Who Built Wealth Over Time

Many people assume that financial success requires a huge salary or insider knowledge. But the truth is far simpler: consistent, disciplined investing often beats flashy moves or perfect timing.

Take Grace Groner, for example. She wasn't a Wall Street titan or hedge fund manager – she was a secretary. In 1935, she invested just $180 in three shares of Abbott Laboratories stock. Instead of cashing out during market fluctuations, she let the investment grow. Over the decades, through reinvested dividends and stock splits, her small purchase quietly turned into a fortune of over $7 million by the time of her passing in 2010.

Similarly, Ronald Read, a janitor and gas station attendant, amassed an $8 million fortune simply by investing in blue-chip stocks, reinvesting dividends, and staying the course. He didn't get lucky. He didn't take big risks. He just stayed consistent for a long time.

These examples may come from the US, but their core lesson holds true for UK investors too.

Here in the UK, stories like these may not always make headlines – but they're quietly unfolding all around us. For instance, Terry Smith, now one of Britain's most respected fund managers, started with a long-term, quality-first approach that everyday investors can mirror. And many ordinary people who've been regularly contributing to a Stocks & Shares ISA for the last 15-20 years – investing in simple global index funds – have built six-figure portfolios without ever picking a single stock.

What all of these investors understood is this: small, smart decisions made consistently can generate real wealth over time. The trick is resisting the urge to tinker, panic, or chase the latest trend. In investing, boring often wins – and patience pays.

Avoiding Get-Rich-Quick Schemes

The allure of fast money is powerful. Social media is rife with self-proclaimed "gurus" promising instant riches through day trading, crypto speculation, or high-risk ventures. The reality? Most people who chase these opportunities end up losing money. Investing isn't about doubling your money overnight it's about making strategic, measured decisions that pay off in the long run.

Remember the dot-com bubble of the late 1990s. Investors rushed to buy shares of any company with ".com" in its name, believing the internet boom would make them overnight millionaires. While some early adopters did see short-term gains, many lost everything when the bubble burst in 2000. The same happened with the housing market collapse in 2008 and, more recently, the cryptocurrency crashes of 2018 and 2022.

The truth is, wealth isn't built by jumping on every new opportunity – it's built by sticking with a solid plan. Some of the most successful investors don't try to predict the next big winner – they focus on strong businesses, invest consistently, and give their money time to grow.

Chasing quick wins often leads to quick losses. But a steady, long-term approach? That's where real, lasting wealth is made.

How to Stay Patient and Consistent

Patience is one of the hardest virtues to practise in investing. In a world where instant gratification is the norm, the idea of waiting 10, 20, or 30 years for significant wealth can feel daunting. But the investors who embrace patience are the ones who see the greatest rewards.

One way to maintain patience is by focusing on the bigger picture. Instead of checking your portfolio daily and stressing over short-term fluctuations, set clear, long-term goals. Are you investing for retirement? To buy a home? To create generational wealth? Keeping these goals in mind can help you stay committed, even when the market is volatile.

Another key strategy is automation. Many successful investors set up automatic contributions to their investment accounts, ensuring that money is consistently being put to work. This removes emotion from the equation. When investing becomes a habit rather than a conscious decision, it's easier to stay the course.

Finally, consider historical market trends. Over the past century, despite wars, recessions, and financial crises, the stock market has continued to grow. While there have been downturns, patient investors who stayed in the market through turbulent times have ultimately come out ahead. The S&P 500, for example, has delivered an average annual return of about 10% over the long run. That means even during periods of uncertainty, those who stay invested tend to recover and benefit from long-term growth.

Adapting to Life Changes and Market Shifts

Investing isn't just about numbers and charts it's about life. Your goals, responsibilities, and financial priorities evolve over time, and so should your investment strategy. Whether navigating a market downturn, adjusting for different life stages, or planning for retirement, the key to long-term success is adaptability. A rigid approach won't serve you well in an unpredictable world, but a thoughtful, flexible strategy will.

Investing Through Recessions and Economic Uncertainty

There's a moment in every investor's journey when the headlines turn bleak, markets plunge, economies slow, and the future looks uncertain. During these periods, fear grips investors, and many scramble to sell their holdings. But history tells a different story: downturns aren't the end of wealth-building; they're often the beginning of the greatest opportunities.

Take the 2008 financial crisis. Stocks tumbled, and portfolios took a beating. Yet those who stayed the course or better yet, bought more when prices were low, saw massive gains in the decade that followed. Warren Buffett's famous advice captures this perfectly: *"Be fearful when others are greedy, and greedy when others are fearful."* The investors who took that to heart came out ahead.

But surviving a recession isn't just about holding on it's about being prepared before one even hits. That means keeping a portion of your portfolio in stable assets like bonds or dividend-paying stocks, maintaining an emergency fund, and avoiding excessive leverage. Smart investors also recognise that market corrections are normal; the S&P 500 has experienced dozens of downturns but has always rebounded stronger.

For those looking to capitalise on uncertain times, consider companies with strong balance sheets, resilient cash flow, and a history of weathering economic downturns. These businesses often recover faster and continue delivering value long after the storm has passed. Recessions test patience, but they also reward those who focus on the bigger picture.

Adjusting Your Portfolio as You Age

Investing at 25 looks very different from investing at 55. In your early years, you have time on your side. Volatility isn't a threat; it's an opportunity. That's why younger investors often lean toward stocks particularly growth stocks with high potential upside. Short-term fluctuations don't matter as much when you have decades to ride out the waves.

But as you approach midlife, priorities shift. Financial responsibilities – buying a home, raising children, planning for university – call for a more balanced approach. This is where diversification becomes crucial. Instead of going all-in on high-growth stocks, a well-rounded portfolio might include index funds, real estate, and bonds to smooth out market swings while still allowing room for growth.

Then comes the transition into the later years, where capital preservation takes centre stage. The goal shifts from wealth accumulation to wealth protection. A portfolio that once thrived on aggressive investing should now prioritise stability and income generation. Dividend stocks, Treasury bonds, and annuities start playing a bigger role.

One key mistake many investors make? Over-correcting. Some shift their entire portfolio into ultra-conservative assets, effectively locking in lower returns and missing out on long-term gains. But even in retirement, you'll need some level of growth to keep up with inflation. The best approach is a dynamic one, where you gradually adjust your risk levels while ensuring that your investments continue to work for you.

Preparing for Retirement: Passive Income and Withdrawal Strategies

Retirement isn't the finish line; it's a new financial phase that requires careful planning. The dream is to live comfortably without outliving your money, and the right withdrawal strategy can make all the difference.

One of the most time-tested approaches is the 4% rule withdrawing 4% of your retirement savings each year to ensure a steady income while preserving enough capital to last 30 years. While it's a useful guideline, it's not a one-size-fits-all solution. Market conditions, lifestyle choices, and unexpected expenses can all affect your withdrawal rate.

That's why diversifying income streams is essential. Relying solely on a retirement account can be risky, especially in years when the market underperforms. A mix of passive income sources—such as rental properties, dividends, bonds, or even part-time consulting—adds stability and security.

Real estate, for instance, has long been a favourite retirement income strategy. A well-managed rental property can provide steady cash flow with minimal effort, acting as a hedge against market downturns. Dividend stocks work similarly, generating income without requiring the investor to sell off assets.

Another key factor? Tax efficiency. In the UK, accounts like Stocks & Shares ISAs and Self-Invested Personal Pensions (SIPPs) offer significant tax advantages. Withdrawals from a SIPP are typically 25% tax free, with the remainder taxed as income, while ISAs allow for tax-free growth and withdrawals at any time. Planning ahead – strategically drawing income from different accounts to minimise your overall tax burden – can help stretch your retirement savings further (similar to how US investors manage withdrawals from traditional and Roth IRAs or 401(k)s). Ultimately, a well-structured retirement plan isn't just about money; it's about freedom. The ability to travel, spend time with family, and enjoy life without financial stress comes from making smart investment decisions long before retirement begins.

BEYOND MONEY: INVESTING IN YOURSELF

When we think of investing, our minds immediately jump to stocks, real estate, or business ventures. But the most valuable investment you'll ever make isn't in a market it's in yourself. True wealth isn't just about numbers on a balance sheet; it's about knowledge, personal growth, and the ability to create opportunities that outlive economic cycles. The most successful investors understand that their financial success is directly tied to their ability to learn, adapt, and think differently.

Financial Knowledge as Your Greatest Asset

Warren Buffett, one of the world's most successful investors, famously said, "The best investment you can make is in yourself." He wasn't talking about buying stocks or real estate he was referring to acquiring knowledge. The financial landscape is constantly shifting, and those who don't evolve with it are left behind.

Consider the difference between someone who blindly follows investment trends versus someone who understands economic principles. One might chase the latest stock tip, hoping for a quick return. The other studies market fundamentals, analyses trends, and makes informed decisions that lead to sustainable wealth. Knowledge is the dividing line between speculation and strategy.

The great thing about financial knowledge is that it compounds just like money. The more you learn, the better your decisions become, reducing risk and increasing the likelihood of success. Reading books on investing, understanding how tax laws impact your earnings, and staying updated on global economic trends give you an edge that no stock tip ever will.

And knowledge isn't just theoretical it's practical. Consider someone who understands the power of compound interest early in life versus someone who doesn't. The first person starts investing small amounts in their twenties and retires comfortably. The other waits until their forties, trying to play catch-up. The difference? Awareness. Financial literacy isn't just an advantage it's a necessity.

The Intersection of Investing and Entrepreneurship

The skills that make a great investor often overlap with those that define a successful entrepreneur. Both require strategic thinking, risk management, and a keen sense of opportunity. In fact, many of the world's most successful business leaders Elon Musk, Jeff Bezos, and Richard Branson didn't just invest in stocks; they built businesses that changed industries.

Entrepreneurial thinking is one of the most powerful tools an investor can develop. Instead of just looking for opportunities to invest in, entrepreneurs create them. They see inefficiencies in the market, identify gaps, and develop solutions. Even if you never start a business of your own, adopting an entrepreneurial mindset can transform the way you invest.

Take real estate, for example. A passive investor might purchase a rental property, hoping for appreciation and steady rental income. An entrepreneurial investor, on the other hand, finds ways to maximise returns perhaps by improving the property, leveraging short-term rental opportunities, or developing partnerships that enhance profitability. The difference lies in vision and execution.

The best investors don't just look for returns; they look for ways to create value. Entrepreneurship and investing aren't separate disciplines they're two sides of the same coin. When you invest in developing skills like negotiation, leadership, and strategic thinking, you're not just improving your ability to manage a business; you're strengthening your ability to navigate markets and seize financial opportunities with confidence.

Why True Wealth Is More Than Just Numbers

Money can buy comfort, security, and freedom but true wealth extends far beyond financial statements. It's about creating a life of meaning, purpose, and impact. The most successful people aren't just rich in assets; they're rich in experiences, relationships, and personal fulfilment.

Think of the investor who spends their life chasing financial gains but never learns to manage stress, build meaningful relationships, or find a sense of purpose. They might have millions in the bank, but if they're burnt out, isolated, or constantly anxious about market fluctuations, are they truly wealthy? Contrast that with someone who has built financial security while also prioritising health, personal development, and a strong network. The latter will always have a greater sense of stability, regardless of the market's ups and downs.

Money is a tool, not an end goal. If your investments don't allow you to build the life you want, then what are they really for? Financial success should enhance your life, not consume it. Investing in yourself means prioritising well-being, lifelong learning, and the ability to adapt. It means understanding that wealth is holistic – it's not just about how much you earn but also about how fulfilled you feel along the way.

At the end of the day, the most valuable investment you can make isn't in stocks, real estate, or businesses — it's in your ability to think, learn, and grow. When you invest in yourself, every other investment you make becomes smarter, more strategic, and more fulfilling.

The path to true wealth isn't just measured in pounds or dollars; it's measured in the impact, wisdom, and opportunities you create along the way.

Your Investing Action Plan: A Recap for Moving Forward

Whether you're just getting started or already dipping your toes in, here's your step-by-step checklist to help you invest with confidence.

1. Build Your Financial Foundation

☐ Make sure you have an emergency fund (ideally 3-6 months of expenses).

☐ Pay off high-interest debt (especially credit cards or loans).

☐ Set clear financial goals—short, medium, and long-term.

☐ Decide what you're investing for: retirement, a home, freedom, or something else?

2. Understand Your Risk Profile

☐ Reflect honestly on your tolerance for risk – how would you feel if your investments dropped 20% tomorrow?

☐ Match your investment strategy to your time horizon.

☐ Remember: risk isn't just about volatility – it's also the risk of doing nothing.

3. Choose the Right Accounts

☐ Open a Stocks & Shares ISA to invest tax-free.

☐ Consider a SIPP for long-term retirement savings with tax relief.

☐ If you've maxed out your allowances, research General Investment Accounts – but be mindful of tax.

4. Pick Your Investment Strategy

☐ Decide: passive (index funds) or active (picking stocks/funds — or a mix)?

☐ Understand asset classes: equities, bonds, property, alternatives.

☐ Consider low-cost, diversified ETFs to start.

☐ Don't overcomplicate it — simplicity wins.

5. Set Up Regular Contributions

☐ Automate monthly investments to stay consistent.

☐ Start with what you can afford — £50/month is enough to begin.

☐ Increase your contributions as your income grows.

6. Stay Tax-Efficient

☐ Use your full ISA allowance each year (currently £20,000).

☐ Understand how capital gains and dividend tax work in taxable accounts.

☐ Use your SIPP to benefit from tax relief and long-term growth.

7. Monitor and Review (But Don't Obsess)

☐ Review your portfolio once or twice a year – not every week.

☐ Rebalance if your asset allocation drifts too far off target.

☐ Don't panic during downturns – stick to your plan.

8. Keep Learning and Evolving

☐ Stay curious – read books, listen to podcasts, and follow trusted sources.

☐ Avoid hype and herd behaviour.

☐ Focus on your goals, not someone else's.

9. Be Patient and Stay the Course

☐ Trust the process. Investing is a long game.

☐ Time in the market beats timing the market.

☐ Celebrate your progress, even the small wins.

Final Word:

You don't need to be an expert. You just need to start, stay consistent, and keep learning. You've already taken the first step – now keep going.

CONCLUSION

Investing can still feel like something reserved for the well-connected — a world where you need insider knowledge or a finance degree just to get started. But the truth is simpler: the biggest barrier to investing isn't knowledge or money. It's hesitation.

The best time to start? Yesterday. The second-best time? Right now. Why? Because the most powerful force in investing isn't timing the market — it's time in the market. Every pound you invest today is a seed. Given enough time, that seed can grow into something truly meaningful.

You don't need to be fearless. You don't need to be an expert. You just need to begin. Open an account. Set up a small, regular contribution. Choose something simple, like a low-cost index fund. Focus on the habit, not the headlines.

Markets will rise and fall. Emotions will test your patience. But if you stick to your plan and stay consistent, you'll build something that lasts.

At its heart, investing is a long-term vote of confidence — in yourself, your future. and the belief that your money can do more than sit still.

So where do you start? You start now. You start small. You start knowing that even the smallest step is still a step forward.

Taking that first step is always the hardest – but once you take it, you'll wonder why you ever waited.

Before You Go...

Not sure what something meant? We've got you covered.

Here's a simple glossary of key investing terms to help you feel more confident as you go. No jargon, no waffle — just clear, plain-English definitions you can come back to anytime.

GLOSSARY OF KEY INVESTING TERMS (PLAIN-ENGLISH EDITION)

Asset

Something valuable you can invest in—like shares, bonds, or property. Think of it as something that could grow your money over time.

Asset Allocation

The mix of stuff you invest in. For example, 60% in shares, 30% in bonds, 10% in cash. Like a recipe for your portfolio.

Bear Market

When the market drops and people are feeling pessimistic. Picture the market rolling over and playing dead.

Bond

You lend money to a company or government, and they pay you interest. It's like being the bank.

Bull Market

When the market is rising and everyone's feeling optimistic. Imagine a bull charging forward.

Capital Gains Tax (CGT)

The tax you pay on profits from investments outside of tax-free accounts like ISAs. There's a yearly allowance before you owe anything.

Compound Interest

Your money earns money—and then that money earns more money. Like a snowball rolling downhill, it grows faster the longer you leave it.

Diversification

Not putting all your eggs in one basket. Spreading your money across different investments to reduce risk.

Dividend

A slice of a company's profits, paid to shareholders. Like a "thank you" for owning part of the business.

ETF (Exchange-Traded Fund)

A bundle of investments you can buy like a share. Great for beginners and brilliant for spreading your risk.

FTSE 100

A list of the 100 biggest companies on the London Stock Exchange. Often used to track how the UK stock market is doing.

Fund

A ready-made basket of investments. You buy in, and a manager (or computer) takes care of the rest.

Index

A list that tracks how a group of companies is doing. Like a scoreboard for the stock market.

ISA (Individual Savings Account)

A tax-free wrapper for your savings or investments. You can put in up to £20,000 a year, and the gains are yours to keep.

Mutual Fund / Unit Trust / OEIC

A traditional UK-style investment fund. Think of it like pooling your money with others and letting a manager choose the investments.

P/E Ratio (Price-to-Earnings)

A tool to help work out if a share is good value. High = expensive, low = maybe a bargain (or maybe trouble).

Rebalancing

Tuning up your portfolio so it stays in line with your goals. Like realigning the wheels on your car after a long journey.

Risk Tolerance

How much risk you're comfortable taking—both emotionally and financially. Your "sleep at night" level.

SIPP (Self-Invested Personal Pension)

A pension you control. You choose the investments, and the government gives you tax relief to help your pot grow.

Share (or Stock)

A small slice of ownership in a company. If the company grows, so might your investment.

Volatility

How bumpy the ride is. Some investments jump up and down a lot. Others take a smoother path.

Thank you for reading So, You Want to Start Investing?

We hope this book gave you the clarity and confidence to take your first step toward growing your financial future. Whether you've set up your first ISA, picked a fund, or simply started thinking differently about money, you're already further ahead than you were yesterday.

Explore More

This book is part of the **SO Book Series** – a growing collection of short, practical guides for real-life challenges. Each title is designed to be read in one sitting and returned to whenever you need a little nudge.

If this one helped, you might enjoy:

So, You Want to Stop Procrastinating

Discover all current titles, updates, and extras at: **SOBookSeries.com**

Printed in Dunstable, United Kingdom